TRAIN DANCE

TRAIN DANCE

Jonathan Wells

12/30/11

For Diana,

These may be different from the poems you remember but I hope they can provide some small pleasures. No test either...

All Best,

[illegible]

FOUR WAY BOOKS
TRIBECA

Please direct all inquiries to:
Editorial Office
Four Way Books
POB 535, Village Station
New York, NY 10014
www.fourwaybooks.com

Library of Congress Cataloging-in-Publication Data

Wells, Jonathan.
Train dance / Jonathan Wells.
p. cm.
Poems.
ISBN 978-1-935536-14-7 (pbk. : alk. paper)
I. Title.
PS3623.E4695T73 2011
811'.6--dc22

2011004077

This book is manufactured in the United States of America and printed on acid-free paper.

Four Way Books is a not-for-profit literary press. We are grateful for the assistance we receive from individual donors, public arts agencies, and private foundations.

This publication is made possible with public funds from the New York State Council on the Arts, a state agency.

Special thanks to the Jerome Foundation for its generous support of this publication.

Distributed by University Press of New England
One Court Street, Lebanon, NH 03766

[clmp] We are a proud member of the Council of Literary Magazines and Presses.

CONTENTS

ONE

TWO

THREE

FOUR

ONE

THE DREAM LINE

In my bottomless bed I am driving
the lamp side of the river to the station past the dog run

and the Tudor Town Hall. The streets waxed slick
with rain are ready for hoodlums in leather

to spook them. Commuter on the dream line,
I can trace seven streams with my fingertip into

the estuary bottom through unfigured air where the river
spreads its fingers into the Sound. An innocent scull rows,

sixteen knees and elbows, a fraction of a centipede going slow.
I wait there and the train plunges through me,

an unscheduled truth rattling. I can choose my seat
by the rain-stained window and fit a magazine to

my face but no matter how far I lean into those turns,
I cannot catch tomorrow's train tonight.

STATIONS OF THE NIGHT

When the soprano leaps through her arpeggios
and other voices fly from their rooms
When scavengers cart the empties off
for five cents each
When the streetlight glows through the shutters
like gold through schist and the fan blades
launch a carousel of shadows
When the television mixes face and text
When the street makes no sound at all
and repeats itself
When doves start as feathery as dawn
and the paper strikes the frail door
When the sheets stick with sweat
and no handkerchief has been invented yet
for disbelief and the body still tingles
with astonishment at what it has
and hasn't kept
When the lamps switch off at seven a.m.
the lips of the night turn blue.

MS. MAGELLAN®*

At first her voice was consensual and pure,
slim adjectives modified simple directions,
miles passed like mosquitoes in the rear view mirror.
"A slight right," she urged, without cadence or rhyme
as we plowed through fields of artichoke and cherry.
She clucked and tutted and chimed her assent,
reading our questions, releasing our doubts, down to
the ocean spread with meteors like mail from space.

Then, by accident, we turned off without her guidance.
She sputtered, recalculated. We heard her pause,
her lips pursed in navigation, their sound lengthening,
thinner, not annoyed, but less committed to our journey.
Her numbers gyrated and spun, the names of the freeways
spilled from her mouth in a mumble of syllables.
When we asked again she chanted agreement and,
her breathing before us, we headed south with the wind.

On the bluff through veils of fog, cedar, rock
and fence, she was silently reasoning, trust restored.
Mistress of the dashboard, she was the goddess's cool
echo, clear and bright like the immortal mother
who outpaddles the drowning currents of the brain,
brave guide to all roads, before then and after.
In the tides of sprinkling mist, she left behind
her final tender imperative, "Turn right, here."

* "The Magellan® Navigation System offers full color, detailed
mapping with clear and friendly voice prompting."

FOR THE SICK

Until you can stretch the shrunken tunnel of sunlight
Back into its normal shape then walk across the street
In its brilliant clothing, you are a child again
In your mother's care, the cool heel of her hand

On your forehead, her ordinary perfume unique,
Cough syrup, opaque, stuck to books you just imagine.
Your knees ache and the vaporizer recreates
A summer at the shore, surf draining through

High-pitched clapping stones. People pass your bedside
But the well are like performers in an equestrian ballet
Vaulting on and off the horse's back for no reason,
Riding under the belly between matched limbs.

Frogmen light your murky dreams with headlamps
And a man jumps from an aeroplane, pulling the cord
Of his parachute so he can reach your bed in time
To pin the details of your mission to the pillow.

You attempt your assignment in the dark but my leaps
And starts make you lose your place in the adventure.
Take a sip of your elixir, dip your hand into the flame
Of steam rising from your machine and humidify us both.

ANOTHER ONE

"There is only each one of us like a cave." *Pessoa*

In each one of us there is another one
who cups a votive candle   who praises the ocean
who lives inside her poem   who rests
who hums   who fingers the trigger
who never laughed   who laughs . . .
who retreats   who joins in   who separates himself
who hides   who is released and hides again
who stands outside the window and watches
his family eating dinner
who sits outside at night in winter
who releases his love and enslaves his son
who grieves for all his mothers
but shows no signs of it . . .
and there is another one who writes it down
who erases   who conceals the seed of feeling
who says it is not his   who adds one plus
one plus one to make another one.

NEARSIGHTED

The forest turns soft and gilded.
Time elasticates: hours, minutes
exchange identities of measurement.
The eucalyptus trees knock hollowly
together. Their sound is an ocean
of sound played through bamboo flutes.
The only danger I provide.

I provide the thief closing
his quick hand: money, identity
tricked away. I provide a red cyclone
of dust that ropes my feet.
And I provide a cop to chase the thief
through a grid of unlikely streets
and a phantom dancer swirling her soiled skirts
of light who leads me safely away.

In the city, glasses on, I am refocused,
under mountains of men with deadpan faces,
streets relearned, the neighborhood thief,
the cars bare their noisy teeth like curs.

~~~~~~~~~~~

My room fills with safety's kindness.
The plaster is not cracked, the ceiling
is unbroken. The titles of my books
are blurred but their meaning is clear.
This is what I come here for.
~~~~~~~~~~~

ALEXANDER'S LIBRARY

I dreamed I saw Alexander's library the night I slept
in the Alexandropoulis station, with *War and Peace*
as my pillow, five hundred miles too far north,

waiting for the train to Istanbul. I was the boy orphaned
on such an afternoon who wandered to the ceremony too numb
to feel the kite string's coil tighten on his white finger.

My kite could soar higher than all the wisdom in the scrolls
my father had once commanded me to study;
the believers and the satirists, historians of the early wars,

even higher than the minds of the stars' geometers.
All those who claimed to live closer to the gods
with their bickering and mastery, I could surpass.

I watched the pageant but I was numb to its colors;
the silver threads in the ladies' skirts, their daughters
holding pinwheels up to the shingled light as the young

boys ran alongside with tinsel. Smoke drifted from
the harbor in the animal shapes of clouds tinted the pink
my grandmother painted on her cheek, and the Emperor,

his eyes still sharp from the foundry, watched the horses'
mimicking steps and the scribes as they measured the bites
from their figs. My kite glided through the sky higher

than the monument, roofless and silent, and I released
it between the tapered pillars that nearly touched in
that upper heaven where parallel lines meet.

A POEM GOES MISSING FROM HIS COLLECTED WORK

His poem about the bakery in Paris with its white
tile, fluorescent light, and the alchemy of its ovens
disappeared from its archive. And the baker with flour

on his cheek and small petals of dough on his arms
and apron vanished too. The baguettes he baked
for his immigrant customers, loaves of a promised life,

were skimmed from the city's surface, removed from
the strange streets that cut through the roots of buildings.
Had I only imagined the poem as bread for their benefit,

the epiphany and leavening, confected it myself, offered
it as a gift, a wish for them who had lost their own rivers
and streets, their languages, their mothers and fathers?

Had I written the poem myself and slipped it in
among his work and had he blessed it not knowing
it was there because it bore his voice? Then, it reappeared

in memorable ink, just three lines, a triplet of hope
between the transport trains and the mind soloing
back, the poem itself nearly gone like all his ghosts—

the river flowing again in its old direction, his first
alphabet like sugar on his lips, and the parents still
sleeping in the same bed they slept in the night he fled.

THE POET'S HOROSCOPE

You will awaken this morning
as flushed as her steaming body stepping
from bath water, as full as the blossoms
on the crab apple tree, each bud globed
in a bulb of water, a raindrop sustained.

A golden retriever will lead you
back from your battle to a garden
you've never visited before that you know
flower by flower, gangs of ferns, a high
forehead of stone, the owl's woodwind
question. You will stand there apart,
in grace, in a footbath of moonlight.

Small incidents will nudge you
from your sleep tonight: the raccoon's eyes
flashing like reflectors without a body,
black tea leaves leafing again in boiled
water, turned a living brown and green.

The day will pay you in dollars for words
that survive the night, the ones that disturb you,
hang above your eyes like bats, make you
turn on the lamp and reach for your water glass,
swelling the brain like a river gathering
more and more rain, the words you repeat
until the meaning warps.
You will guard them as you sit shrinking

at your desk, poet, paper thin and paper filled,
palpating the painted wall for its water pipes.
In these rooms, flecks of paint will be
your only color.

In your next life you will be a builder of reservoirs
and dams, and sleep with your dousing stick.
In your next life you will be patient and tall.
In your next life you will hardly care for words at all.

PATTERNS OF SLEEP

America falls asleep from East to West
toppling like whole forests in an ice storm.
Some children are seized in their last syllable,
others are conquered by a book.
In the hall a single lamp holds its vigil,
the moonbeam is a post of light.

At the coasts the oceans toss and turn
brushing the tangled beach with regular strokes.
Inland, fields of corn sway like sea fans
in a trance of water. The mountains
bewitch and stupefy the body,
deserts spin the brain to sand.

I defend the citadel of sleep as the world's force
assaults me with messages and mail, the rains
of heaven and local rain, dawn sketched
freehand between the terraces and rooftops,
until the sun swells up over the threshold
like a Sunday paper thick with news.

YOGA DOG

Good morning. Take the right hind leg and stretch
it straight behind you. Farther. Now replace.

Left one please. Behind. Farther. Now replace.
Scrape the chest down against the carpet.

Extend the neck, chin out, rocking on your hind legs.
Again, lifting a rear leg. Either one. Linger there.

Now, the other one. Excellent. Now lift the tail,
no the tailbone, lower the sternum to the carpet.

Feel the carpet rub against your fur. Good.
Stretch a front paw out and let the body relax.

Thirsty? Take a drink. Shake the leg out, next,
the other one, let the neck hang. Close the eyes.

Now a meditation. Imagine you are walking
to the park, you feel light and airy, your muscles loose.

There is a little chill in the air but your coat keeps
you warm enough. Another schnauzer comes along.

You sniff each other in a friendly way.
Your lead lengthens. You seem to like her.

It is mutual. Very good. Now she starts
to trot away but something is restraining you.

What is it? A memory, a dream or just the leash?
Let the mind go. Travel to that time and place.

TWO

THE TAILOR'S SONG

If I could cut my own cloth

With my own pinking shears

So it fell just so, harmonious

Across the shoulders, sweeping

From the seat to the knees,

Melodious in the sleeve,

Verses flowering like

Handkerchiefs, then I could

Carry myself like a tune

Into the chorus of the city.

SHARING THE SUN

Blossoms and red berries crowd the sky,
the sidewalk closes down and I am shrunk

by my little foreclosures, a reduction of
hat and coat and gloves to shirtsleeves

and a pair of shorts perhaps, a short walk
through flannel layers of air to the park

where cardinals plot their nests with feathers
and string. Vague tugboats in the distance

say they will mother me and the towns
across the river promise to be my harbor.

The breeze is fragile again and the sun, all
busyness in the kitchen, fixes a meal

of almonds, plums and leaves. Through
the strainer of the trees I hear a salsa band

playing a *rumbita* and then burst into
the "57th Street Mambo." I follow it along

good paths to where they stand in a bunch,
the brass rhythm melting in their hands.

Only a few girls dance bravely there together
to raise the stakes of awe the river wind

feathering their hair.

MORNING GAMBLERS

They look through me as if I had not lived
yet in my shapeless suit, my unwrinkled shirt.

I pass them in the gambling car which rocks
to a syncopated beat, tilts the cardboard table

on their knees, their ties flung back as though
a real wind had stolen in to frisk them.

Slaves and enemies of chance, the dice
their only eyes, the window smudges

winter. Luck streams in blind and blindness
multiplies the towns along the river into a blend

of platforms, mummers' faces and signal towers.
I take my backward facing seat far down

the aisle. The naked beech trees knit
a fence to keep time and chance away

until I take my ticket and slip it back
into the lottery of the city.

ESCAPE ARTIST

As a child I slipped through the knots death tied,
Sidestepped quicksand, picked the locks in time.
When I was older I mourned the child who died.

In Pompeii, I pushed through the gate to hide
On top of a hill that lava couldn't climb,
As a child I slipped through the knots death tied.

Like a sprinter stopped in the middle of his stride,
My feet were rock, my phantom speed sublime.
Ten years after I mourned the child who died.

From the synagogue I heard the mob's horses outside
And flew to the window before the faithless crime.
As a child I slipped through the knots death tied.

The rabbi said we'll burn now and he never lied.
In Babel all tongues abandoned their rhyme.
In middle age I mourned the child who died.

Earthbound or stone no self will be denied
Taken face by face in our mutual prime.
As a child I slipped through the knots death tied,
When I was older I mourned the child who died.

LONDON PLANE

When I'm alone the tree I love whispers
and calls to me, indifferent to the season.
I come to her in spring when she's in bud
and winter when she's naked,
only one side warm. In fall,
she forgets herself
and dreams.

I come to her for learning and read her bark
like braille. Her arms are twisted,
lifted for attention, glassed
in rain or wrapped in mist
or gray. She speaks from
her own wisdom not always
prompted by the wind.

I come without ideas of love for she
is already rough and rounded,
cankered, tall, and we are
not alone. Finches listen
from her branches and
plastic bags luff, confiding
my desires in the wind.

The tree I love lowers me
from my window ledge,
equal to her height.
She says *Sit close to me.*
When I call to you
what loneliness
makes you listen?

THE EARTH'S HEARTBEAT

I woke to the hum of the mottled night,
shapeless stars splashed across the sky
like wine from a goblet a god had dropped.
As I stood up the table rearranged its legs,

pottery lids rattled in their cracked sleep,
a dream thinned out on the curve of my lashes.
I followed the floorboards' grain, as straight
as railroad tracks across the Plains, like the child's

step upstairs outlining the dark, toes measuring
the carpet. I first heard the earth's heartbeat
not high in my ears but conducted through my feet
along the bass instrument of my body

as if I straddled a buffalo's grave and
its shaggy heart was reborn in the basement,
mammoth and assured. The vibration rose up
through the house and the undulating floor

and touched my own heart sinking and rising
against my ribs like an accordion's bellows,
the perfect movement continuous and deep
like stars waning or grapes becoming wine.

~~~~~~~~~~~

I didn't know that the earth that scintillates
and holds our parents fast in its vaults
had its own moving heart. So we both
depend on that hidden contraption,
~~~~~~~~~~~

captain of mood and inclination, beautiful
machine abandoned by a god in a fit of
distraction after a banquet of grapes and wine,
indifferent to the careful paths we took.

The heart's life is a gift dropped off by a stranger
stopping in on her way to another party who
drops back in to retrieve it after she learns
the address was wrong, the people moved on.

~~~~~~~~~~~

The earth's heart still beats for mine.
The stars follow me like the eyes of my father.
But, heart, when I speak with you the words are stronger
and fit better in my mouth than my tongue.

Still, your poem must wait its turn in the queue
of what is unsayable; the red fox rubbing out
his tracks with his tail, the infant's heart
alive today, lifting his first pair of fists,

even the television that looked through me
like winter at the dreamers on the couch
I must chase like smoke through the night,
my heart pounding and my net full of holes.
~~~~~~~~~~~

REMEMBERING NOTHING

for Luc Graham

The morning of his birth is radiant
like the new fleets of cars
and pickup trucks shining on
the dealers' lots, like the clock faces
scrubbed clean and gleaming.
The surfaces are repolished before
returning to their regular sheen.

The books are omniscient,
the letters exuberant and clear,
the grass is renewed and
the lightbulbs are refreshed.
The full newborn moon,
continents and seas commingling,
fades like a white peony bud
at the top of its gangly stem.

The day melts in his mouth
like the first taste of milk.
The infant is a messenger
from the former world whom we
hope for but each cloudy eye creeps
open, remembering nothing.

TRAIN DANCE

At the boarded up station the trains arrive
in fits like manna from a city of feasts.
My son and I wait for them on the platform
and start to sway to encourage them from

the distance. At first he moves slowly, doubtful
that any prayer will make that gray face appear
from the isolations of fog and light like lava.
I say to him if you won't dance too the train

won't come to help him with his hesitation.
So released from any shame of recognition
we dance like crazy minstrels, fingers snapping,
heels and toes bouncing off the glittering concrete,

grinning with our eyes closed like monkeys
handling gold. Our dance of faith gathers speed
like the train itself leaving its original station
as though we were tuned to the same internal

station, an accelerating salsa slow in the waist
amid the throwing of arms and legs until it
stops before us. The doors split open and still
jangling we take our seats bound for plenty.

ON MY LIPS

When she kisses me good night
I think of the kisses not given;
unborn children, white paper,
an ocean promenade of possibility.

The kisses unmade make a poem.
Where else do they belong
if not on my lips.

APOLOGY (FATHER AND SON)

A fire makes friends my friend I said
So sit here and handed him newspaper
To tear into strips and twist and kindling
To lay in squares over the paper and

Three logs to stack in a pyramid.
Hold the match I said while I struck mine
And we touched each end to light our edge
And watched the passing images fade

Like promises in ash. On our faces
We felt heat the same temperature as
Shame and the room rose to contain
Our one shadow that charcoal evening.

THE LAST SUMMER NIGHT

After my son wraps his shoes in tissue
and packs them in his case to go,

the cat's crying splits the darkness into
strips of silence and the house loses its

other music. Rooms lose their furniture
without a sound, paintings are erased from

the walls like lights being switched off,
and the ceiling lifts into the stars' cathedral.

The groping, oceanic night smudges all lines
with its black arms and legs, and so she won't

disturb your dreams that the thin air makes wild,
the cat weeps again for him who will never

quite return. What I hear I hear through
tears. Your back is the wall I cry behind.

DYLAN THOMAS STOPPED IN OSSINING

Even thirteen, riding the station wagon's axle bump
Like a surfboard in the curl of the hills through
The housing clusters, my hair straight on the felt roof,
His every word arose in me as a dove awakening
In a magician's hand from the miracle of thin air.

On what Welsh planet in a cottage did his kiss ring
Against the glass like a tuning fork that reverberated
In my suburb as the cassette's chocolate-colored tape
Unleashed so many feet of language, language retrained
Like a lap dog who slowly learns to hunt and lust.

Mother drove us past the Dew Drop Inn as his tongue
Marinated in richer whiskey liquored on,
The metallic fog hovering over the Hudson River
No match for the cobwebs of Swansea Bay, our modest
Conversation pale next to his livid mastery.

As the tape replayed his plaintive tricks, our car
windows sealed against the flood of other noise
so nothing would restrain that tune in me, and with
no other witness but my self, I believe, wavering,
she carried it too through the patchwork of the hills.

It is his deeper singing I remember
and the adjectives he added to his fear to give it
the best direction. His fears masked hers and made
them orderly like two lanes of traffic merged
in one neat caravan of cars.

A VISIT

My brother sleeps upstairs on an inflatable
mattress (that air was once my breath).

There won't be time before he leaves at
dawn to recall the grapestand under

the stars near Kandahar, or our friend Joe,
emerald smuggler or Green Beret, seized at the border

with Iran, shouting, 'I'm a Christian' as he was
led away by guards to the barbed wire enclosure.

If my brother crashes on the floor, his dreams porous,
awakened now, will he remember the elements

I haven't chosen. Even asleep he offers comfort
without color. He is still here but unconscious

and, gone but conscious, how will we live
again that clear woodsmoke evening.

A summer squall leaves few traces on the lake:
a little air still in the sails, an extra wrinkle in the waves.

ONE LIFE

One life is long enough. Please
don't ask for days or months
or wait until the bottom of the page
to visit the doves she named for you,
the bed she kept made for you, her hair
that grew into your head, her *hush*
that passed your lips.

One life is long enough to remember
what you have forgotten—the attic swings
laughing on their chains, shoe prints on
the ceiling, scrimshaw shadows the pine tree
scratched into the wall's back when the branches
shook, the lantern on the dock blinking
off and on as somber now as a beehive
in winter . . . . All the things
you couldn't pack.

One life is long enough to know
what you've forgotten and will forget
again: the Russian mowers who came
on Saturdays and taught you to say
Dosvidan'ya.
Goodbye.

THREE

GRAFFITI

Our wall ran as long as a freight train
with over a hundred cars of rolling stock
and kept rushing.

We wrote with spray cans, markers,
smoke and gas, flowers and roots,
species of trees, hummingbirds,
eggs and seed.

We used all the languages, parts of speech,
symbol, likenesses and punctuation.

The light was shed from galaxies and candelabra,
flashlights, diodes, temple lamps, tapered bulbs
and crystals.

Every letter was statuesque,
every scratch an epitaph.

THE GIVING POSITION

The poems gave me a house, a boat, two rivers
and a meadow, my mother, my father, sister and brothers
weaving back across an ocean, a lake, a pond.
They gave me fish that didn't blink, acres of
swallowing grasses, some tables of the tides
and the long slow highway outside.

The gifts appeared at dusk in my living room window,
hid in the grist of night. Or I dreamed them
and shed them where the rivers splashed my feet,
walking on its stones or squatting in the hills.
Day by day I pay them back.

THE NAMES

for Arnold Wells

As his name leaves the clothes he filled,
Resides outside the nursing home door next to other
Names whose clothes the mind won't stir
Or whose startled hair the sun won't shine,
Let him lie protected in the charm of his age.
Dry greeting drips from the faucet of his mouth.

Which name, separate from its body, lives on,
Enters another life and lives again restored,
Limber as a dance of ribboned smoke
Laughter complete in its flashing entrance,
Seals his signature with a giant's hand.

NOW CARRIED TOGETHER

Her husband's arteries long iced over,
her parents turned to ash,
Yiddish picked like a wishbone
from her brother's closed throat,
(his poetry a poor defense against the century)
my grandmother came to the cottage door
wearing the wholesome coat my father'd bought.
She still heard the peddlers' tin cups in
her ears years after she stirred romance
at the stove.

The gray brown dog leapt across
the hillside excited for the frail hug
grandma almost gave, knocked her down
to the gravel, and licked the whisker on her chin.
Her crossed eyes wandered to the treetops
which rotated around the sun like a circle
of girls holding hands, turning sideways,
like the high branches she touched from
the grass of her past, supine, next to her sister,
counting wishes.

I went toward her slowly in the black
and white footage that memory preserves.
Careful of her stiffened hair, the wrinkled ripples
around her mouth like extra messages
of effort, she watched me, frightened,
through her catseye glasses as though

I were a doctor without a license, not
her grandson who had run to greet her
at the door and who held her now,
a toppled jay, against his chest.

NEARLY SPIRIT

Nearly spirit, my mother dies again disappearing
while still here, driving through her glass house,

receiving the crowning heads of trees into the valley.
She'll take her shears with her, no use to me, and leave

her palette with all its shades of green.
Her fingers that scooped the soil, roughed my hair,

unhusked the corn and plucked the silk threads out,
clutch her dress. Her eyes implore me to uphold her right.

She fills the scented den, clatters in the kitchen,
roams the greenhouse, a commander of the greenhouse,

a tail of motion following her with a train of motes
like galactic particles trailing their meteor mother.

Watering the orchid from her old can, she confides
that she can feel the tumors push in her like shoots

she can't reach to pinch off their shriveled heads.
That garden is overgrown, the sun doesn't touch

the ground and she shuffles on the cold slate
in a tightened gait unmoved by the sound

of my footsteps as I walk behind her.

BELOVED

Nameless, I wandered into your tent of names
when the small trees of my street couldn't put me
back to sleep. I looked around, I was alone.
The moon fell loosely through the flaps.

You'd said I would be the one who writes it down
like the squaw carving names into her sheaves of bark
as though I knew what other men dreamt.
But I remembered too much and choked.
The wind was gone from my fingertips
and I couldn't unclench my moving fist.

You'd said I could name myself.

I picked up pencils I'd used before
and they seemed like your hands, long and pebble-scented.
I boarded a train to the border of the city
but turned back toward you at the railhead.
I trailed the rounds of your doves
in a changeless circle. The night lost its sense
of touch so I grasped for you again.

You chose my clothes from a hall of closets.
You said I was the sun for a fleet of ships;
the oars, the strokes, the rudder and the wake.

I drove my name into the black ocean clouds
to know if it would stick but the thunder came
and washed our rowboat away.

I was loved by the weather of chance.
At your breast no name mattered.

INDIAN SUMMER

In Indian summer time repeats
like a retold story, the earth stutters

in its rotation, a needle stuck on
a long-playing record until the first frost

opens spider veins of ice
in the sidewalk. The last plums,

cloudy, tender, darken in the market;
daft fingers fumble a cold silver coin.

"In Indian summer," my mother began,
"before leaving on their trip up north,

your uncles brought their blankets back outside
to remember the campfire and the warmth

of the stars. We didn't know when
or if they'd return. Tim came back

different from when he left.
He stayed that way forever."

As acorns shatter on the rooftop
like artillery shells that they will memorize

in their dreams as war, the children
listen sky-eyed as I tell my mother's

story. Unblinking, faces milk bottle clear,
they demand to know more.

Later, on a homeward path, my mother
takes my arm so near to her and says

she doesn't think she can complete
the season. The secondhand wind leaps

from the branches to our coats, nudges us
forward, draws a cyclone of leaves around

our feet. We keep our balance in silence.
Scarlet leaves fall from a single tree

and for a day or so or as long as
the wind is patient, the image

of the phantom tree is refigured
on the flaming grass in its native fullness.

Red leaves run into orange
and yellow streams before lifting away.

In the morning, some are still
caught in the treetops' first baskets

of light and I collect them from there,
while I wait, hopeful, gazing up,

the wind pinned in my caverned chest,
for the rest of the story.

EULOGY AT NIGHT

A truck vanishes from ear to ear,
an airplane soars on a secret mission.
A train, traveling without a track,
blows its bugle through my window
piping me away from the business
of the city.

The poem I repeat for you beats
inside my pillow; your oceans and summers,
weightlessness and impatience.
The words console my mouth
like caramels and along
the garden wall shadows
of the sycamore leaves
dance in a wild ballet,
free of the mother tree.

Your stars are still warm
on this clearest evening,
your questions still scratch
against the dark. The sky is an illusion
of touching lights so ask again,
How many nights are there left like these?

THE HILL ONE YEAR LATER

I wrote myself back into the ceremony of ashes
on the hillside of sliding winter leaves
and sand cherry bushes. A triangle, a chime,
a few notes played on a flute by a child,
the naming of plants, phrases worthless
to the air. Wind without direction.

The hill rose and sank inside my chest.
Each verb took me closer with its pale breath
to this being, the hill's silhouettes of motion,
the life's elaborate agitation.
Each adjective tiptoed in the halflight
to the window, groping for a shadow.

The hill moved me in two directions.
It shrouded me and I broke through it. I rose
against it and I shrank. It towered over me
and plateau'd. Coming was not leaving.
There were two sides to every feeling.

PLEASE HOLD

I am a telephone ringing in mid air,
a chair pushed back from the dining room
table after a long conversation.
Speak to me again. Say my name.
The rice, cold not close, still marries
the bride and groom. The holster
fires like a gun.
The reins of the cottonwood trees go slack
and the field lays down on itself.
Bird songs overlap their notes
in the fluttering.
I am hungry for the earth. Aren't you?
Come to me. Say my name.
The sun made me ten stories tall
when I walked in the lines
of the labyrinth keeper's rake. One story
made me wiser than I am and I could feel
the geese fly out of me although
they barely moved their wings.
Say my name.
The dressing room mirror revealed three lives
in that face but she saw only two.
The horse and child mattered to her,
the other life was mine.
Is that call for me?
Please hold—
I'm coming.

UNTITLED

You taught me the river—
its slender hands, fugitive smile
and phosphorescence.
The river became my blood,
my voice.
Some mornings when the earth smells
of earthworms and mist
a guitar will steal the river's chords
from the underneath of leaves.
A violin
will take its deeper wood,
the catgut strings its notes.

We walk the river
rock to rock, the river shape a fossil
snake in a million miles of rock. The ears,
the mouth, the neck, the bitten palm
of rock watch it go.

Oh, never let me go.

FOUR

THE WELL

When I die please name a well for me,
a well plumbed in rock, the smell of water
on my loved one's lips who I loved from too far away.
Tell her the ripples of leaf-made ships
will reach me one day, adrift.

What does water move? What does it conduct?
Words fluent on her lips? Her eyes glinting black?
I'll hold her as though her body is a raft
made of bric-a-brac and we'll be two swimmers
welded again into the sun on the sea.

Choose a well to bury me in,
slow echoes and a wake to make my bed,
a sunken stone turret, a graft of moss,
and from the upper world, a pebble tossed.

LIKE WATER, LIGHT

Like water, light always finds the opening;
where the door is warped inside its frame,
where the blinds bend in the windowpane,
where the curtains sag just below the railing.
Morning light converges on the ceiling.

Like light, you blaze through all my clothing;
to my silent skin and the tartness on my tongue,
to the pulse rushing in my wrist, the heart remote,
to my heartbeat itself repeating *I am, I am.*
You startled me in the dark then sucked me out.

HIKE TO GRIZZLY LAKE

You do not recognize yourself
but you are there in the passage
between the mountain's shale teeth
and the valley . . . .

In the cavalry of days, neck sweat, sweet
sorghum, heavy packs and horseflies . . .

In the mines' chorus of open mouths, the miners'
cabins now unfolded, brown squarehead nails half-buried
in the brown pine earth . . .

In the high pond itself, a windowpane, an unturned
surface that the ruby-chested trout tips into eccentric
circles . . .

In the drowning light, in the timothy grass where
the spider hangs a silk tightrope you didn't see
until you tilted your head into the sun.

THE MARK

I worry about you tonight when I turn out the light. I shelter
my head in the cove of my arm like a flat-bottomed skiff
that carries your face, not watching, adrift, because there
is no current to bring us closer. You are walking on spongey

blacktop so far away in West Darfur. Haughty camels hiss
and nip. The children as attenuated as the angels in black
and white movies are vanishing. All are restrained in the net
of the sun's cumbersome vines. Here, above four shades of blue

in the slopes of the ocean, the afternoon weather is unclear:
the clouds might be fog, the fog might be leafsmoke.
The children playing Marco Polo in the pool like sleepwalkers
remove your name from my throat's memory. The palm trees

sway as they did on the skirt you wore leaving. The breeze
touches me with the edge of your hand. Clouds suggest
your waist and hips turning back. The same sun drops from
my railing to your waking eyes. The telephone awakens

and through tidal silences swept back and forth like a broom
across the floor, I learn the story of the student who was arrested.
I hear the power failure behind you: the clink of flashlight
batteries, a radio moaning somewhere in the laundry in the yard.

Will you be so alive for me tomorrow?

Night watches me and breathes
its prickly heat. Soldierly shadows march past the curtains
guided by headlights. Aside from the cat who licks herself
clean at the corner of my bed I am alone and meet no resistance

in the air. Tomorrow morning is another mouth to feed.
You hoard against you the bodies of children as light
as bird nests, several at a time. Old women just thirty drift
toward the well to rinse off death's traces but the skeletons

of husbands and cows lie too close to the surface to forget.
Gunmen who are only eyes watch from camelback,
helicopters fire blindly on foragers and collectors
of firewood and those who lost the bearings of their grief.

~~~~~~~~~~~

You arrive home late and your luggage is much too light.
"I gave everything away," you say. "They told us not
to cry for them." So you kept your tears for me to hide
with the other treasures of our lives. You imagine that

the merciful world of bandages and nurses, poultices
and morphine, seeds and hoes, sorghum, paper, crayons
and soldiers, hospitals and tents will not fail to notice them.
Perhaps you don't notice but you who left our safety behind

to see for yourself, to love outside yourself, have joined
the tribe of witnesses and victims, and like the warrior
who the war never leaves, now carry the mark of those
who own no more than the mist of their next breath.
~~~~~~~~~~~

SPEECHLESS

Our love makes no speaking sound
Like the feather a magpie lost
Silent on our frozen ground.
After the moods and states we crossed

We arrived here too late for words
Though we'd believed in them before.
Burned in, conjured up or overheard
They are not inside us anymore.

Where they echo, ease, begin,
Snared in the jungle of your unlit hair,
Dim in the stem of your hidden ear, skin
And senses replace the spoken air.

And, with the missing feather found,
Will the magpie feel the wind above the ground?

IN GRAND CENTRAL STATION SOME MOMENTS WITHOUT POETRY

I hold my hand up to the high window
looking for the hidden threads
as if it were a fifty-dollar bill.
I must be disappearing.
The faces of boys are lost
inside the cheeks of men,
their footsteps are lost between the stars,
and the stars, too far apart
in the manmade sky, are green
and brackish.

I remember lying down
but don't remember what I was dreaming.
My dreams taste murderous and sweet
at the corner of my eye.
I stand very still for them
but they just rise up like ashes.

Others move away from me,
they must know that I am waning.
Train shadows derail in tunnels
on subway tiles and pillars,
Their brakes are crying, over
and over, the same lament.
I hear it faintly and pick it up;
it spreads like a whiskey fire.
The silver escalator rises up
to higher floors of observation.
The vaunted heavens clarify.

Give my hands and fingers back,
my sandals and my sailing feet.
Take my coins and overcoat.
Tie me up, extort me, but lead me back
to the life I had just taken.

THE FUTURE

I wanted to be everywhere at once
without a shadow, as though motion
might be my anchor and my shape
a spinning bullet miles above the earth.
The sun didn't catch my quickness
and I skimmed the world's surface
picking up fruit without stooping.

I want to stay here now in every room
of her house, one fresh with lavender,
another cooled by pearls, the table set
with silvered fruit, a bunch of red grapes
in a pewter bowl, the light carried by flies
across a sumptuous emptiness.
I don't watch myself,
I have no shadow.

I met a man
who sat in the sun so long
he could remember how deep
the day could be in him
and he sank into his shadow
which ate into the grass
and he became my father.

SAIL FOR US

In his bedroom, the kite leans idly
against the desk despite the cycles
of wind that settle on our meadow in sets
like waves. In the closet, her nightgown
has hung on the hook too long, forgetting
its question, and, in my mirror, I measure
how much love is left in my eyes, my face.

Although we are warm in the armor
of these walls, sail for us
through the Malacca Strait while
the radio transmits alone, reaching its own
frequencies, to the Andaman Islands where
the orange fish are scooped up from the sun's
path of coals and hummingbirds cling
to the flamboyant bush, changing
color in mid air.

SUMMER MASK

In the blizzard she wore a mask
of pleasure and stepped so
carefully on the slate.
Her smile was beautiful
because it asked for nothing.
The dogs barked at the Buddha
on the sparkling grass as though
there were no other gods for them
or strangers to surprise.
It was summer again
if only briefly
and the river passed
its shallow tears.
The maple leaves swayed
to the mildest breeze
until the snow made it
hard to see.

THIEF

I will take another bone
from the radiator of her ribs
until every bone is gone
and her heart irons my heart
smooth with its sibilant heat
and her hunger fits my mouth
with hunger for the morning.
Her breathing is my fortress.

One by one I'll put the bones
and fire back yet the flavors
will linger in my senses until
the comfort becomes a need
like the rhythm of the seasons
the body receives and uses
as its reason the way a deliberate
hand lifts the fork away from
the dying bees in autumn.

So like the boy upstairs in his bed
comforted by the after-dinner voices,
the rounded whiskey notes,
the humming approbation,
the open-mouthed relief of people
safely in their places, I replace
the borrowed faith before
anything was missing.

CABOOSE

On a night outside time I heard wind chimes
dimly ring, then rest and a train accelerate

like the rhythm of slow maracas gaining
on a sad old Cuban song. I didn't know until

the afternoon that there were no cabooses
anymore, that the train, however long, carried on

without its tail, a rattlesnake without its rattle.
I guided it, born for me on Christmas morning,

through shrubs of wrapping paper, down the steep grade
of a wooden slide, past my mother's early morning rapture.

No caboose where the conductor could discuss the matter
with his pipe, display the flags, fuss with ticket stubs,

empty the windsock of dust and rain, wave to the boys
on their bicycles waiting at the junction for the unknown

to stop and let them board.

ACKNOWLEDGMENTS

Alaska Quarterly Review, Atlanta Review, Carquinez Review, Crucible, Eclipse, Edgz, Epicenter, Evansville Review, Flyway, Harpur Palate, Hayden's Ferry Review, Hurricane Review, Iron Horse Review, MacGuffin, Meridian Anthology, New Delta Review, Nimrod Journal, Phantasmagoria, Poet Lore, Quiddity, Rattle, Red Wheelbarrow, RiverSedge, South Carolina Review, Westview, and *Yalobusha Review.*

With love to my wife Jane and family, Alexander, Juliet, Delilah, and Gabriel.

Deep thanks to my readers for their thoughtfulness and patience.

And to my teachers for their guidance—Marie Ponsot and Christopher Merrill.

Thanks to everyone at Four Way Books.

This book of poems is dedicated to my mother, Jean Wells Wallace.

Jonathan Wells's poems have appeared in *Hayden's Ferry Review*, *The New Yorker*, *Poetry International*, and other publications. He edited *Third Rail: The Poetry of Rock and Roll* (MTV Books) which was published in 2007. He lives and works in New York.